What's In The Ocean?

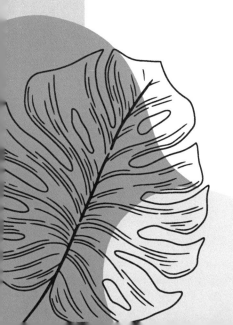

This book belongs to:

- -

- -

- -

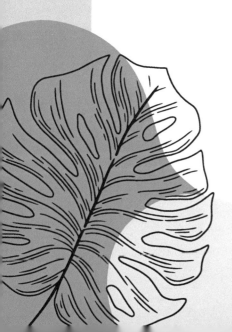

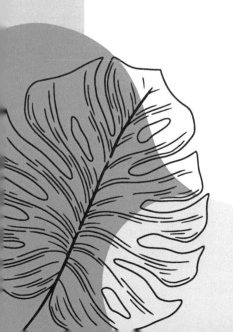

Once upon a time, in a land where the waves kissed the sandy shores, there was a curious little turtle named Tommy. Tommy loved to explore and discover new things, especially in the vast and wondrous ocean. And so, the tale of "What's In The Ocean?" begins.

One sunny morning, as Tommy swam near a colorful coral reef, he met a wise old seahorse named Sebastian. With a gentle smile, Sebastian greeted Tommy and said, "Hello, little one! Are you ready to learn about the marvelous things that reside in the ocean?"

Tommy's eyes sparkled with excitement. "Oh, yes, Sebastian! I want to know everything about the ocean and its treasures."

Sebastian nodded and began their journey through the deep blue sea. As they swam, Tommy marveled at the coral reef, where bright corals formed a magnificent underwater garden. "What are these beautiful structures, Sebastian?" he asked.

"These are coral reefs, my young friend," replied Sebastian. "They are homes to countless sea creatures, providing shelter and protection. Their vibrant colors make the ocean even more magical."

Moving on, Tommy spotted a school of dazzling fish with shimmering scales. "Look, Sebastian! What are these graceful swimmers?" he asked, enchanted by their beauty.

"Dear Tommy, Those are fishes," answered Sebastian with a smile. "They come in various shapes, sizes, and colors. They swim together in harmony, creating a breathtaking spectacle. Some are fast like the sailfish, while others are vibrant like the clownfish."

As they ventured deeper, Tommy caught sight of a gentle giant gliding through the water. "Oh, Sebastian! What is that enormous creature?" he asked, filled with awe.

"My curious friend, That is majestic whale," Sebastian explained. "They are the largest animals in the world, and their gentle nature touches the hearts of all who encounter them. Whales sing beautiful songs that travel across the ocean, filling the water with their melodic voices."

Further along their journey, Tommy noticed a group of playful dolphins leaping and twirling in the waves. "Sebastian, who are these joyful acrobats?" he inquired, unable to contain his excitement.

"They are dolphins, Tommy," replied Sebastian. "They are known for their intelligence and playful nature. They leap and spin through the water, bringing laughter and delight to all who watch. They are great friends of humans and always ready for an underwater adventure."

Their adventure did not end there. Just as Tommy and Sebastian continued their exploration, they discovered a hidden treasure along the ocean floor. They found a collection of beautiful seashells, each one unique in its shape and pattern.

"Look, Sebastian! What are these marvelous treasures?" Tommy exclaimed, his eyes widening with delight.

Sebastian smiled and said, "Those, dear Tommy, are seashells. They come in various sizes, colors, and patterns. They are gifts from the ocean, washed ashore for us to discover. Seashells carry the stories of the sea and make beautiful keepsakes."

Tommy carefully collected a handful of shells, feeling the smooth texture and listening to the whispers of the ocean within them. He marveled at their intricate designs and vibrant hues.

"These seashells are like treasures from a hidden world," Tommy whispered, his heart filled with wonder.

As the day drew to a close, Tommy and Sebastian arrived at a mysterious underwater cave. Tommy gasped as he saw tiny, glowing creatures illuminating the darkness. "What are these magical lights, Sebastian?" he asked, amazed.

"They are bioluminescent creatures, little Tommy," explained Sebastian. "They possess the extraordinary ability to produce their own light. Their twinkling displays create a mesmerizing spectacle in the depths of the ocean, guiding lost travelers and sparking wonder."

Tommy's heart swelled with joy as he realized the vastness and wonders of the ocean. He thanked Sebastian for the incredible journey and promised to continue exploring and protecting the ocean's treasures.

And so, dear little friends, whenever you visit the beach or dip your toes in the ocean, remember that beneath the sparkling surface lies a world full of marvels. Coral reefs, colorful fish, majestic whales, playful dolphins, and magical bioluminescent creatures await your discovery. Just like Tommy, keep your eyes wide open, and let the ocean's mysteries unfold before you, for it is a treasure trove of wonder and enchantment, waiting to be explored.

Made in the USA
Las Vegas, NV
18 December 2023

83163922R00024